this POCKET TRASH/art sketchbook

for bad drawings only!

belongs to

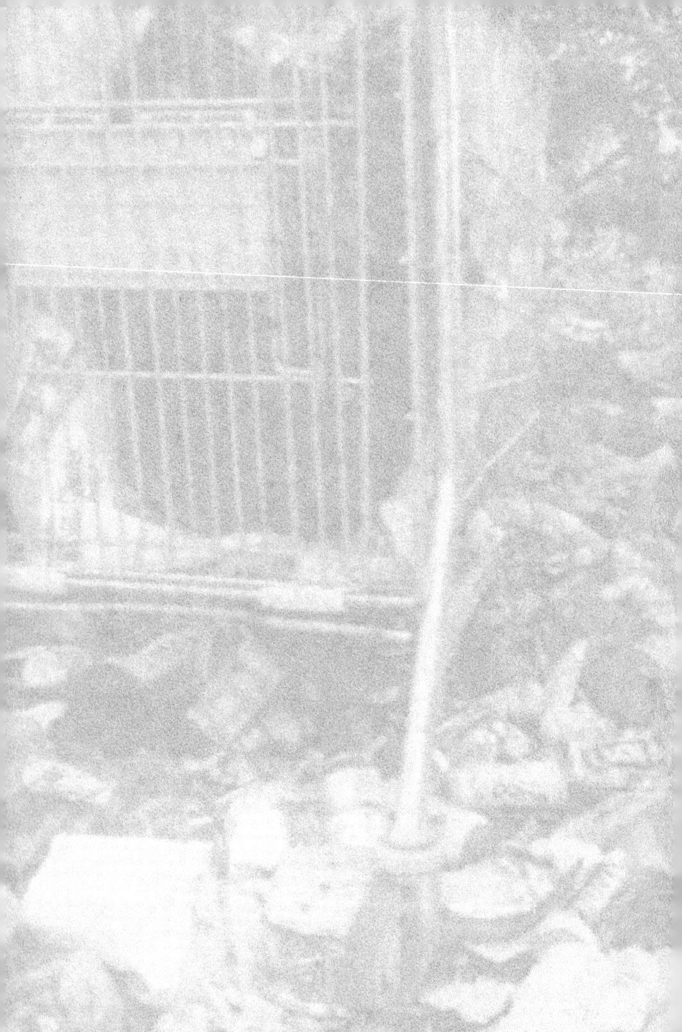

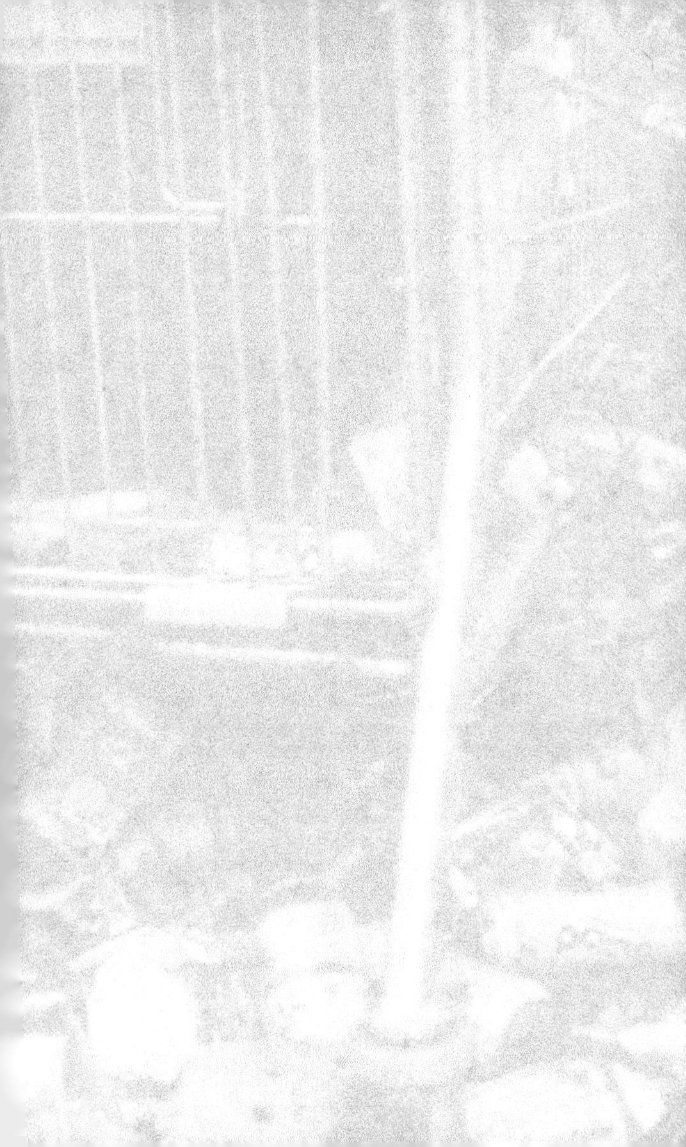

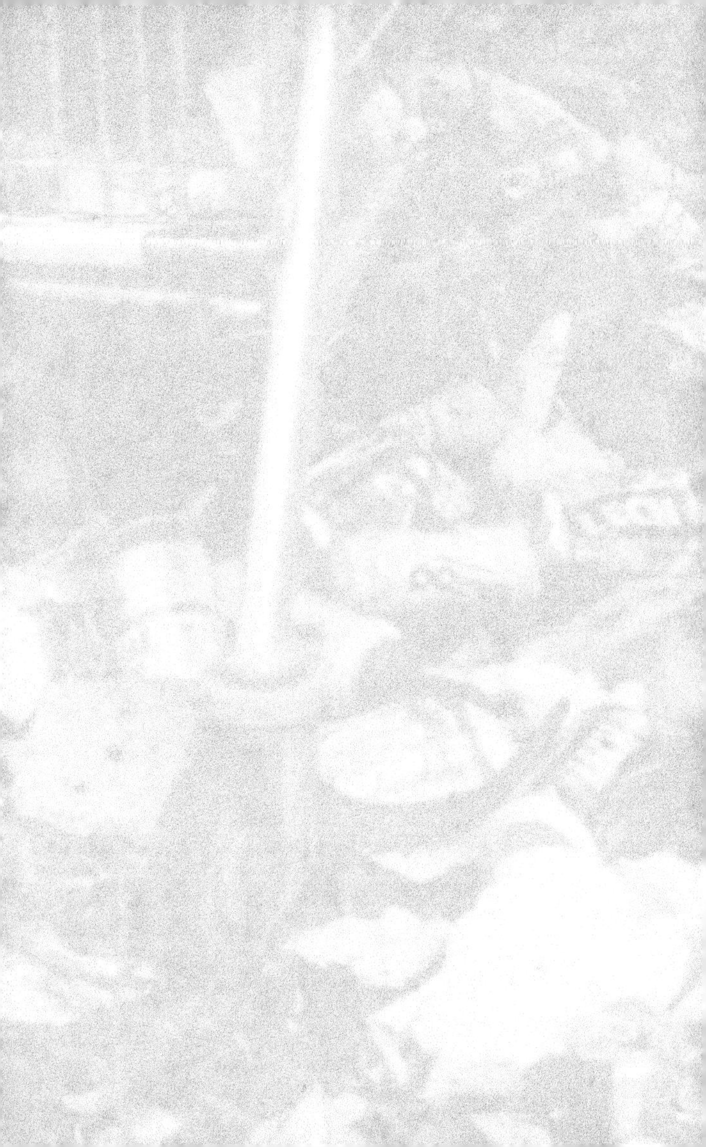

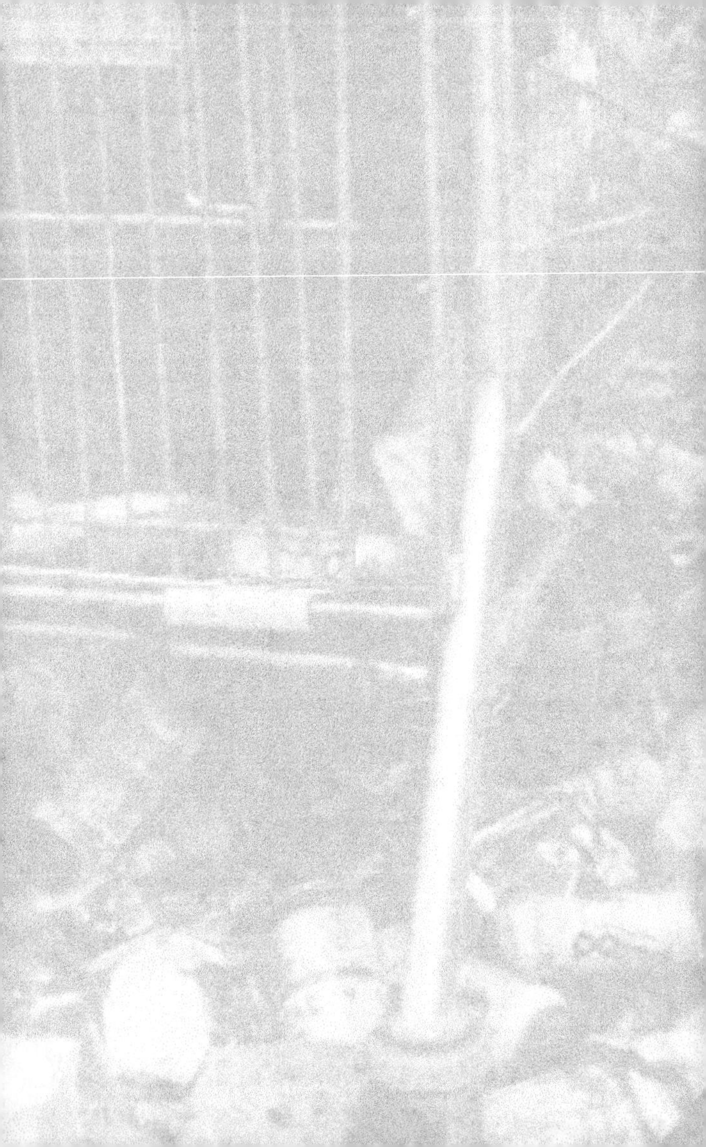

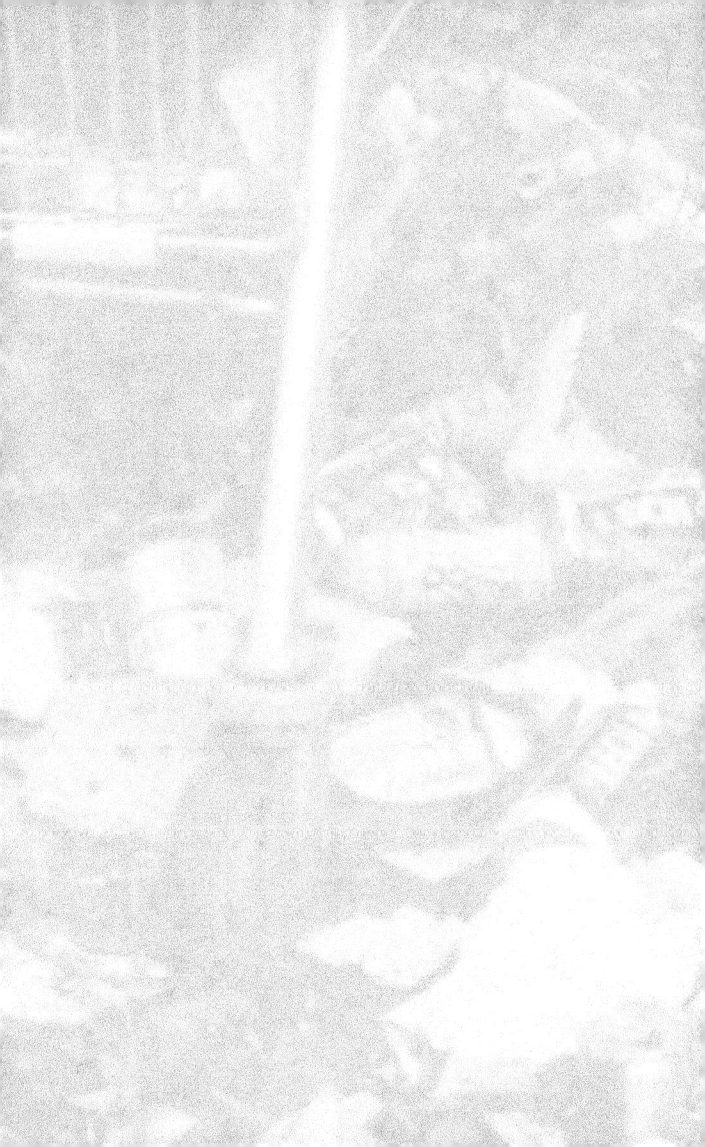

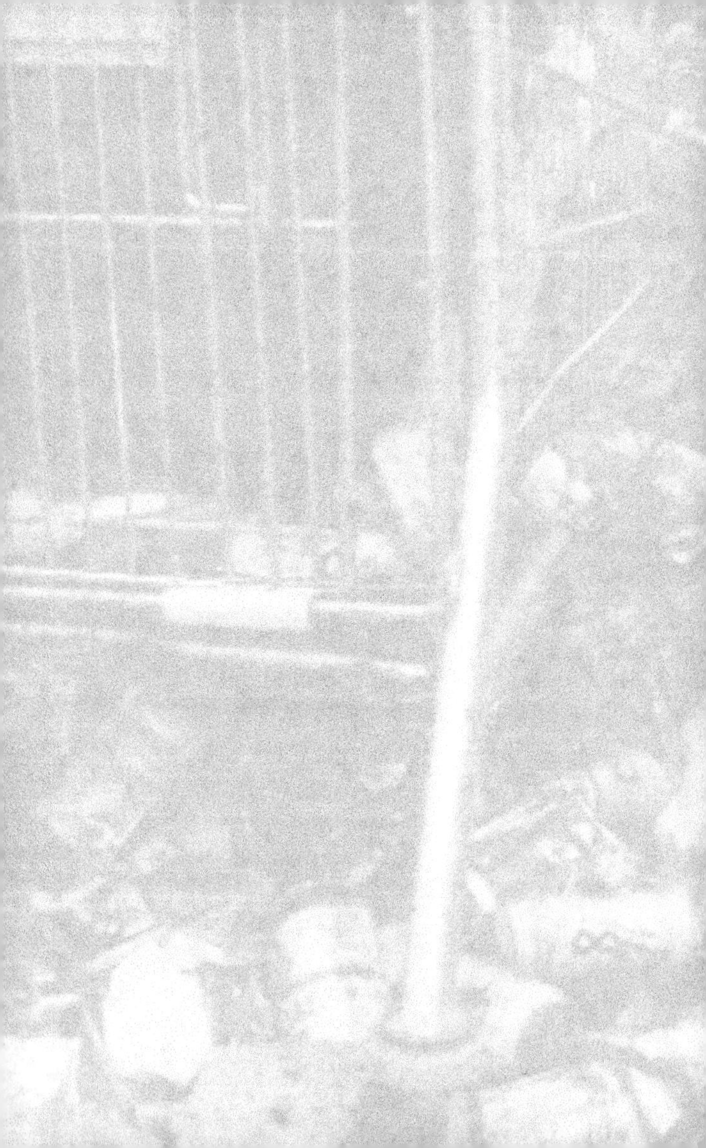

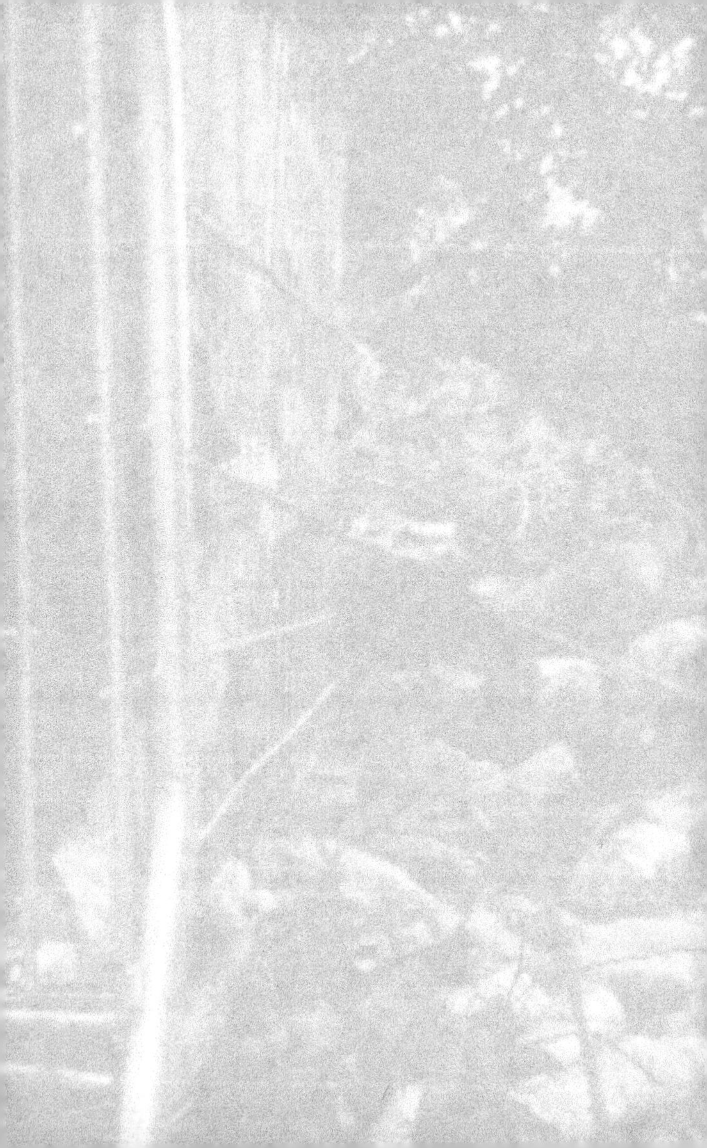

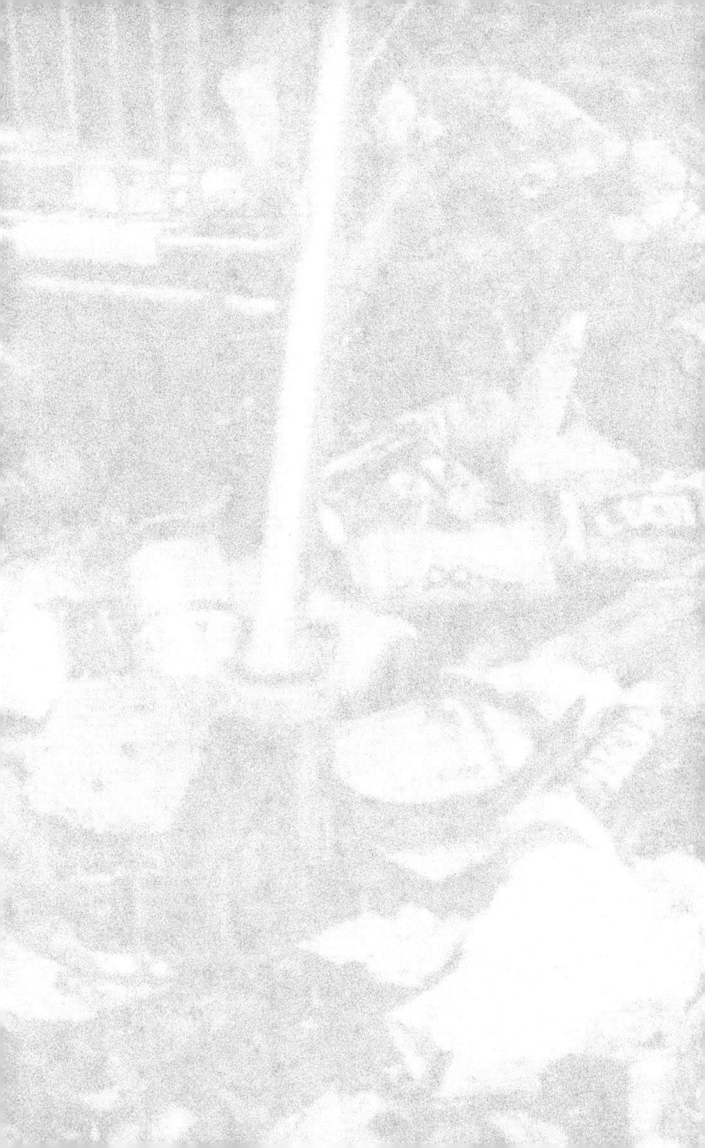

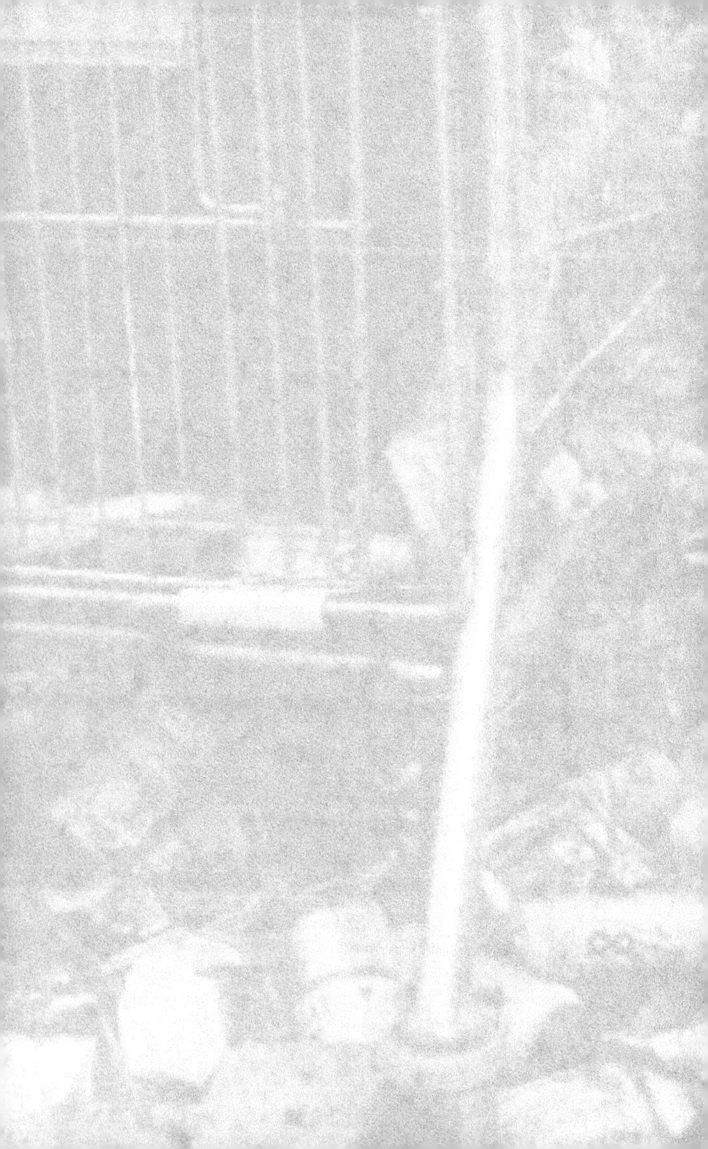

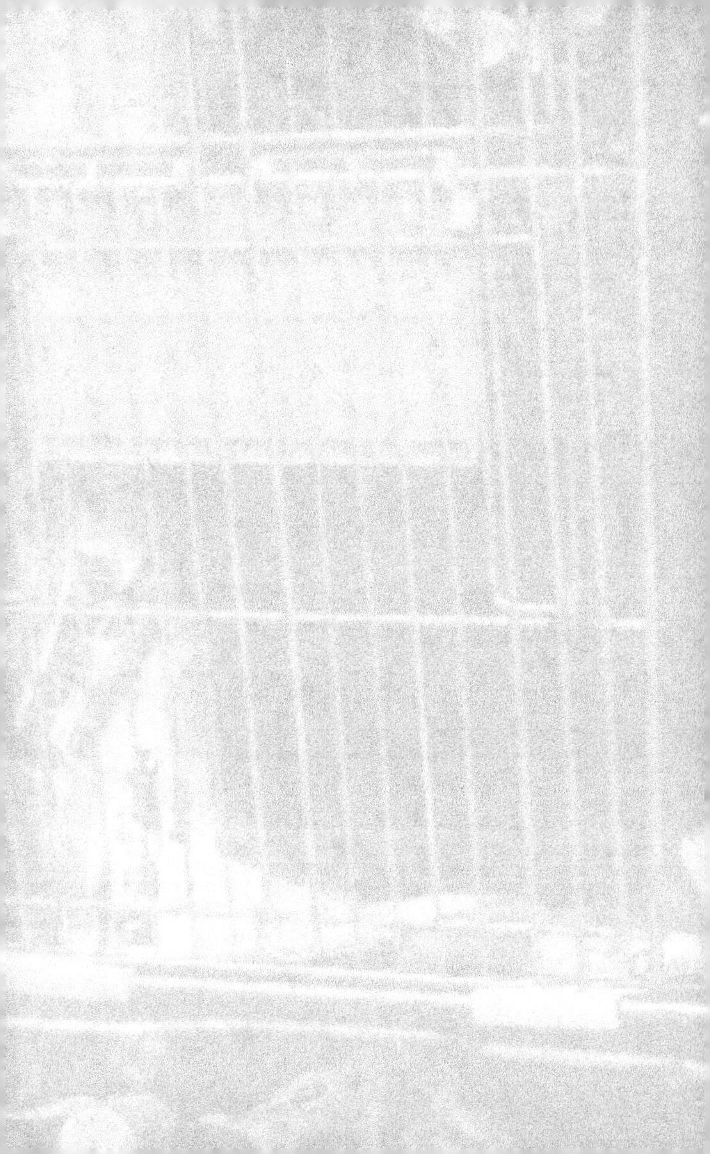

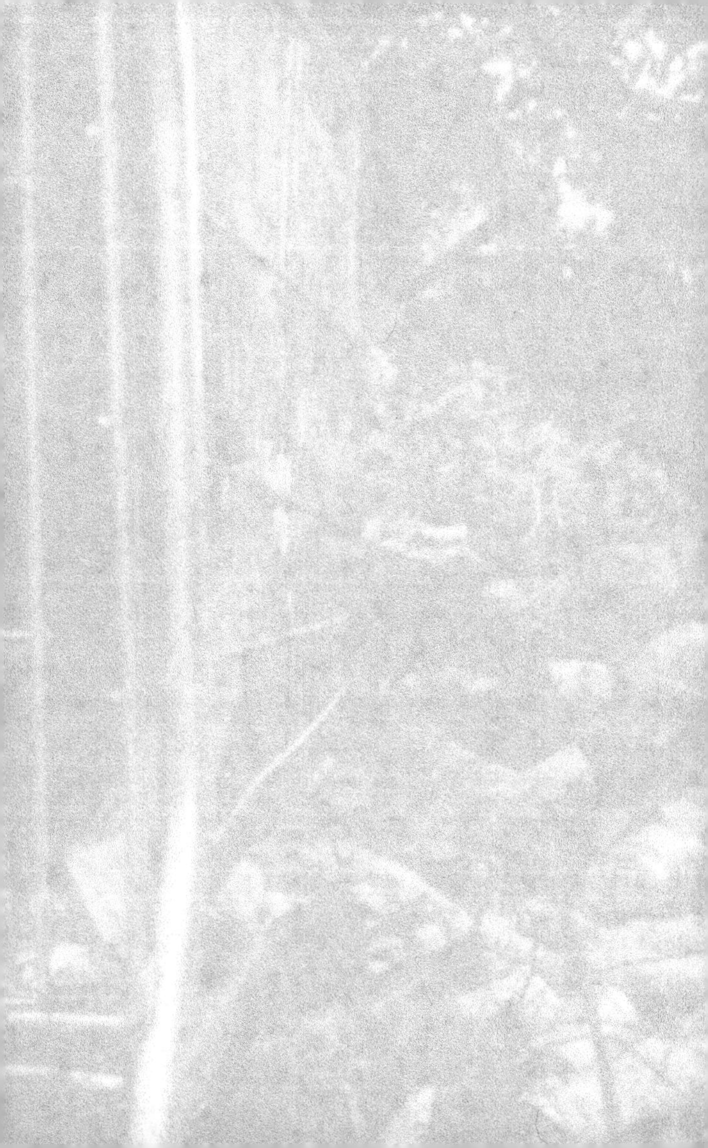

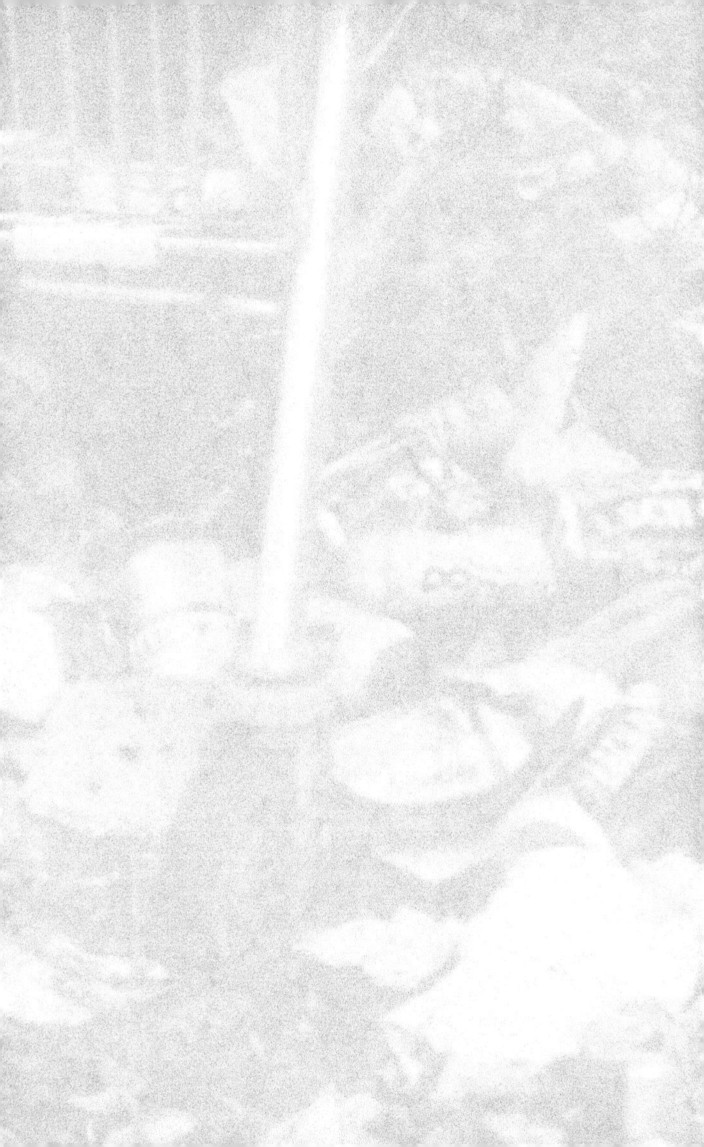

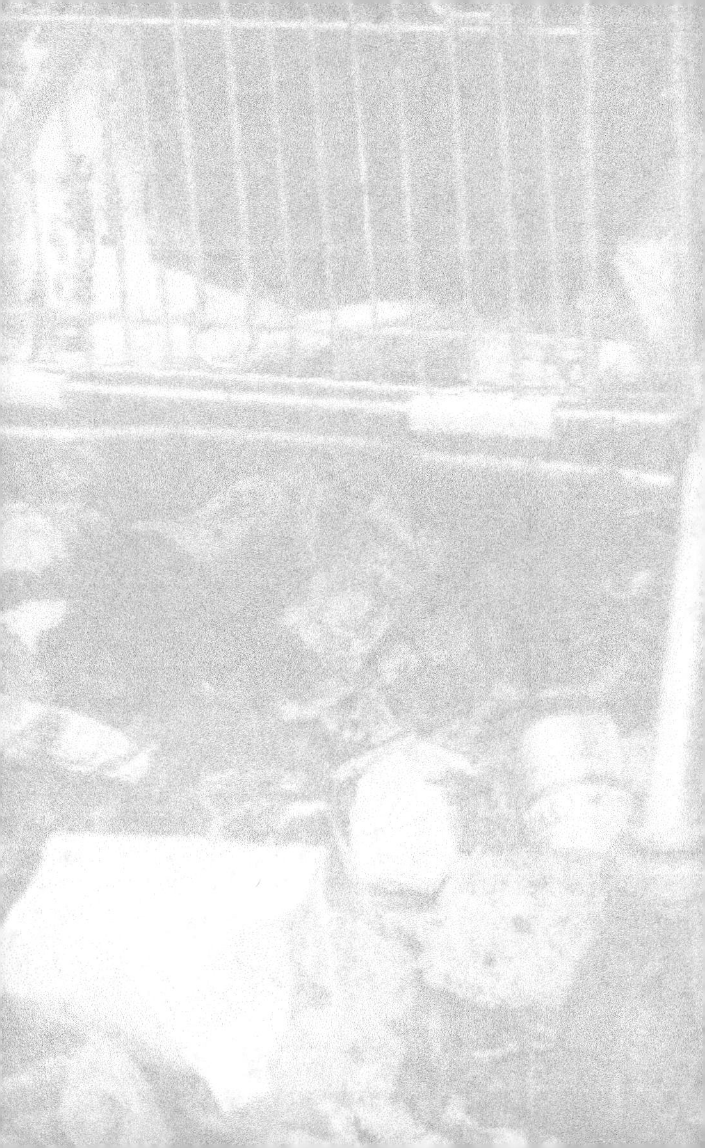

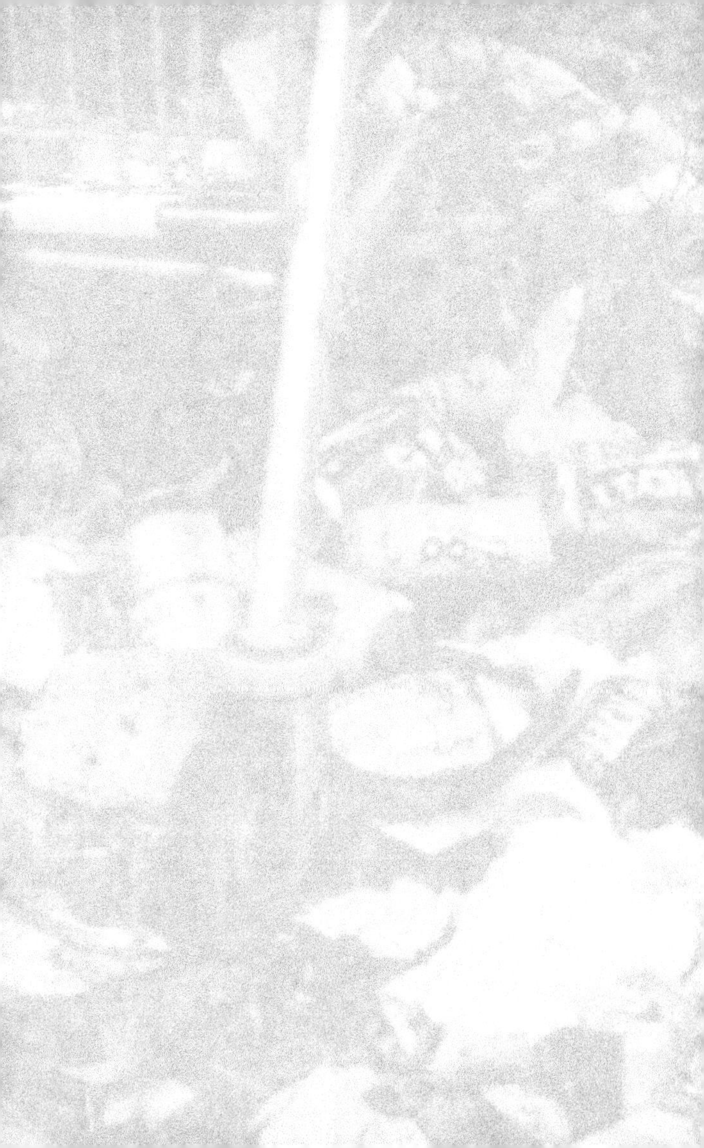

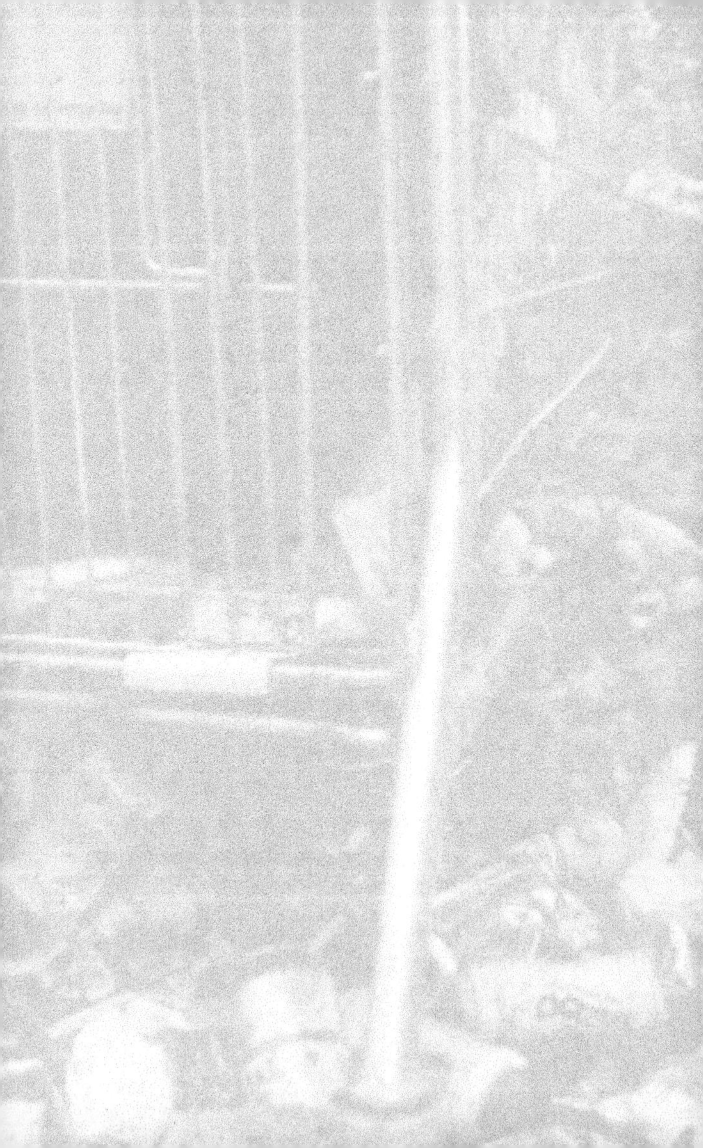

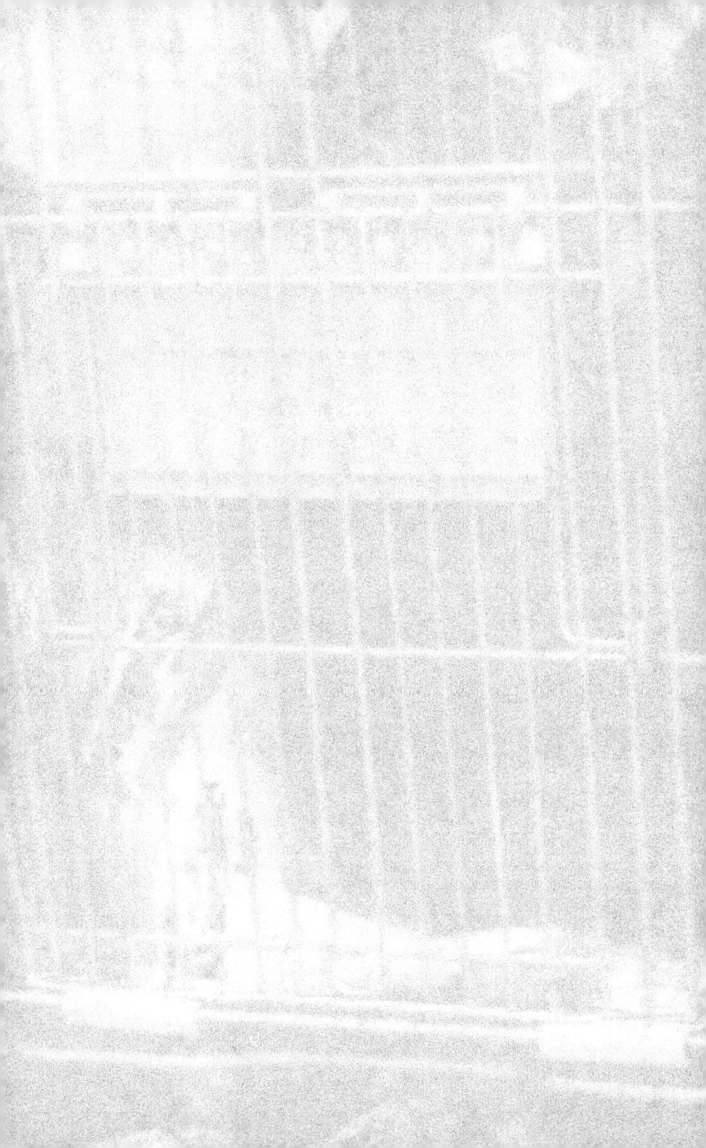

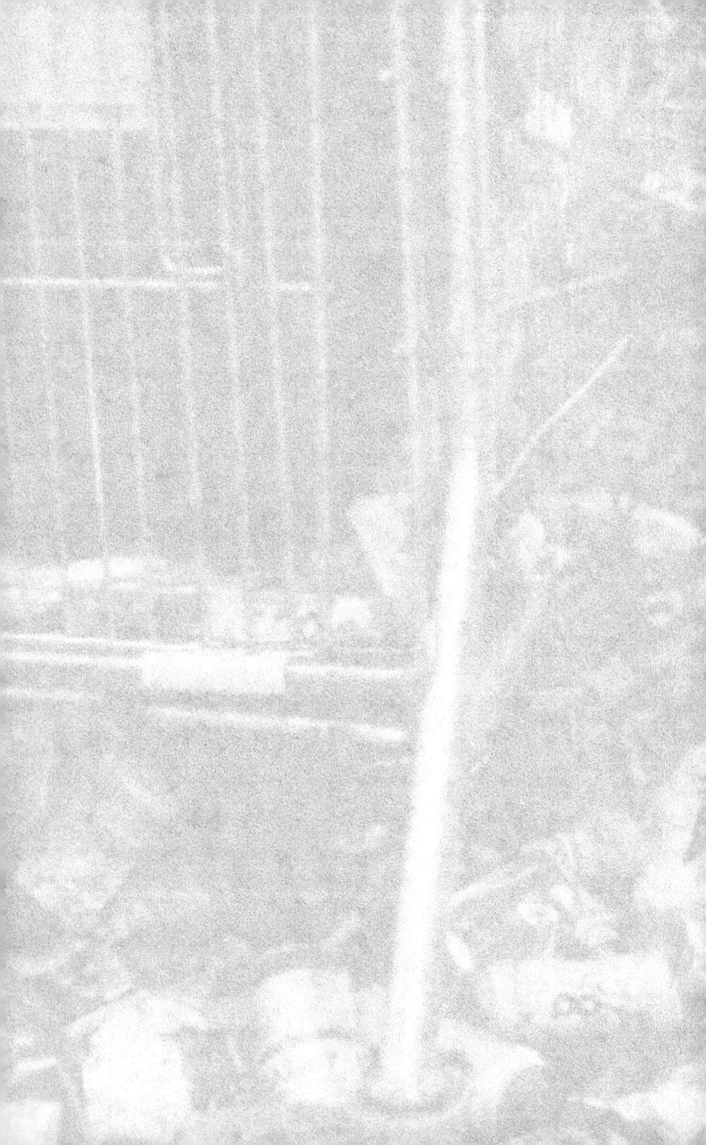